The Spiritual Covering

To order additional copies of this book, contact:
Xlibris
1-888-795-4274
www.Xlibris.com
Orders@Xlibris.com

Designed by Freepik

ISBN: 978-1-7960-9437-4 (sc)
ISBN: 978-1-7960-9436-7 (e)

Print information available on the last page

Rev. date: 03/13/2020

The
Spiritual
Covering

What to look for in a man, as it relates to marriage.

Re'Dina L. Frazier

Chapter 1

First thing first, God isn't going to send you a man who›s unable to provide for you and protect you.

The man who is sent to cover you, will be able, in that moment, to provide and protect you. It won't take years for him to get into that position, he'll already be there. "A man with a loose spine is no different than a snake" ~Darius E. Frazier. If he's a weak man who is indecisive and doesn't take care of his responsibilities - he's not God's best for you. Period.

Marriage doesn't began when the vows are spoken in front of witnesses.

Marriage begins when two people are brought together by the prompting of the Holy Spirit. Note: this doesn't have to be in a religious setting. We meet people daily in various venues.

The Holy Spirit will usher the person who is assigned to you into your life at the proper time. So there's no need to keep asking God when will He send you a man.

The Holy Spirit will direct your footsteps towards one another - it will direct your paths to each other, by situations and circumstances. And yes, even in those unfortunate moments where you're thinking God has abandoned you. It's in these moments that God is orchestrating something far better for you. You need only to trust the process.

Loss your job - trust God. House foreclosure - trust God. Car repossession - trust God. Divorce pending - trust God. Health failing - trust God. Have to relocate - trust God. Didn't get that promotion - trust God. Loss of a close love one - trust God. Simply put - whatever it is, trust God enough to know that He has your best interests at heart.

Chapter 2

God knows how to bring two people together, in His perfect timing. So you don't have to rush into anything. Take your time, slow it down, because you have a lifetime to get it right with the right one.

The two shall become one. Let me say that again. The TWO shall BE-come ONE. For some reason there are many people who do not understand that concept. The two becoming one doesn't include in - laws, Ex - lovers, sisters, cousins, or friends. Nor does it include Tyrone, or Tynesha when things at home aren't going well.

When it's God there won't be any priming, or forcing the situation, or manipulation of the circumstances- things will simply fall into place effortlessly. So come on up out of those bushes, Girl. Stop stalking him to see if he's cheating on you. Trust me, the man God has for you won't give you a minute of doubt as to where you stand with him. The chosen man for you will solidify your position in no uncertain terms. It'll be up to you to know how to play your position.

Conflict: There will be conflict, because the enemy doesn't want two Believers, or two praying individuals to come together. Why? Because one can put a thousand demons to flight and two, ten thousand demons to flight. See, if Believers were to be joined in a matrimonial union, it would be a great threat to the kingdom of darkness. Expect disagreements and days of no communication between you both during the courtship phase, but you'll come back together - if it's by divine design. No relationship is without its hiccups. Trust, he'll be missing you just as much as you're missing him.

And truthfully speaking, every relationship needs space. It's alright to go a few days without talking to your love interest. It'll give you both time to reevaluate your life and your relationship and give you time to spend with family and friends doing things you enjoy with the people you love.

Chapter 3

God, is omnipotent, all powerful, able to do, or be whomever He will. Trust that He has the power to make awesome things happen in your life.

God is omnipresent, everywhere present, there's no height, or depth, or space, or time where His presence doesn't exist. Trust that He will be with wherever you go and in every situation you find yourself in.

God is omniscience, He's a all knowing God. There's nothing done under the Heavens that He doesn't know about. Trust that He knows all that there is to know about you - He knows what you need and who you need in your life.

God is The Almighty Father, certainly He knows the person who is a better and more deserving fit for us; And how and when to bring that person into our lives, also knowing how to bring two people who are meant to be together back together when there is a conflict.

He knows all our flaws, everything that we try to hide from others around us. He knows about our weaknesses and every tear we cry secretly.

He knows and is most familiar with that little child inside of all of us, who has yet to grow in wisdom. That small child that we will be taking into a marriage.

God knows the right person who will have the patience and endurance for the many temper tantrums, or emotional meltdowns every child experiences.

Chapter 4

Let's talk about the covering: Covering is defined as a thing used to cover something else - in order to protect or conceal it.

The man chosen for you will come into your life knowing his position in your life. He will instinctively know the role he's assigned to hold in your life and act upon it without hesitation.

The chosen one for you will be willing to compromise for the better good of the relationship. He will always seek ways to elevate you to become your best self.

He will support and encourage you to be and do your best - he will challenge you to come out of your cocoon. He will have no qualms about celebrating you, nor will he be jealous, or envious of all your accomplishments. In fact, he will be your loudest cheerleader.

He will be the covering, or guardian over you and protect you not only on a physical level, but guard and protect your emotional, mental and spiritual well being - as if his life depended on it. He will gladly and willingly serve and protect you all the days of his life.

God's Protection: God will place a veil around you. Whereas, the man God has for you, will be the only one who can see you. This is God's protection over you, because you are His daughter. God will hide you from predators whose only job it is to destroy you before the man of God can find you. Understand that rejection is protection.

Be thankful for the rejection of others - it was God protecting you. See, when the wrong man comes along he'll only be interested in one thing. This man will only see your outward appearance, he'll only be interested in your performance in the bedroom, or your money, or your living situation in order to see if you're a easy mark. These men prey on empathetic women. Women who are always trying to save the world, but in the process forget to take care of themselves. These type of men are nothing but takers, he's not a giver, he only wants what you have and when he's done using you he'll move on to his next victim.

This is why it's very important to keep busy during your "Lady In Waiting" stage. Because, the enemy will send many distractions in order to keep you from your purpose, or blessings. Remember, all snakes don't slither on their belly - some have two legs. So it's most important to stay vigilant and alert.

Chapter 5

It's imperative that you stay in the presence of God, as not to be drawn away by fleshly concerns. Beit, reading inspirational material, self improvement goals, writing in a journal, working on business plans, or helping out in the community. Whatever you do, stay busy and mindful of your surroundings.

Allowing yourself time for meditation each morning before you start your day, will prove most beneficial in order to regain focus and mental clarity. When we remember to put God first, He sees that as denying the flesh to follow Him. And, He will honor that effort openly. Always keep God first place in whatever you do and He will look out after you. Always. God truly cares about you. There's nothing that you're facing, or pondering that He's not privy to - He knows all and sees all.

Chapter 6

But, How Will I Know That He's The Man God Has Chosen For Me?

The question isn't how will you know - it's how can you not know.

If you take a honest hard look at yourself and realize that you're not the greatest pick of the litter, or the smartest, or brightest, or the most beautiful out of the pack. Or, when you weigh your own pros and cons, and truly see your flaws, or how there's more negatives than positives when dealing with you and the chosen one still chooses to stay around in spite of you - again, how can you not know.

Only the one chosen for you can put up with you - without breaking a sweat. Why? Because he was made for you. He, my darling, isn't a push over, nor is he a weak man. His sternness and boldness will challenge that little girl inside of you to become a full fledged woman. With him, you would have met your match. He will get on your last nerve and cause you to roll your eyes like a Casino Slot machine, but when he's not around you'll find yourself missing his very presence. Because, your soul/spirit knows that with him, is where you belong. Why? Because you were made for him.

You'll find that this one won't be so easily shaken by your antics. And, despite all of your idiosyncrasies, he'll remain consistent with his actions to do you good and not evil. He won't bail on you at the first sign of trouble. His stance with you will be sure and stable. He'll know and understand that no one is perfect, not even he, himself and because of this, he won't try to change you, or judge you.

The chosen man for you will think of ways to please you. He'll come up with things that you both can do together. This could be in the form of long weekend drives, rock climbing, hiking, bicycling, scuba diving, art museums, stageplays, romantic scrolls, dining at your favorite restaurants, or even spending the day with your family. The where doesn't matter, as long as he gets to spend time with you. What separates this unique man from the rest, is that he's more focused on what pleases you and brings joy to your life. Because he sees you in his future, he wants to know everything that will make that future brighter.

But, he won't allow himself to be taken advantage of, or abused in any way by you - he'll have no problem walking away from things, or people who devalue him, or his efforts - and rightfully so. Because he recognizes his own value and knows that he's deserving of the best for himself as well. He is, of course, a man after God's own heart.

Chapter 7

The Purge

Purge: A cathartic release. To rid (someone) of emotional bondage, memories, or conditions.

No one has ever moved on successfully in a joy-filled, peace-filled relationship without purging their soul of toxic energy from a failed negative union.

No one's exempt from a broken heart. At some point, we've all had our hopes and dreams shattered by someone who decided that they no longer wanted us in their life - so they ended the relationship. Some ended on good notes and some on very sad notes. It's life, it happens. Brush yourself off and keep it moving. KIM.

However, there are those soul ties that keep us bound to a person. Whereas, we find ourselves reliving a bad dream over-and-over again. These soul ties are demonic influences in our life. They continue to draw us back to a particular person, even though we know that the person isn't any good for us. Our soul cries out for them when we're apart from them. Even when we break things off for the thousand and one time, we find ourselves aching for them. This Jezebel spirit (spirit of control) attaches itself to us through direct contact with the person- most often through sexual contact. Not all soul ties come through sexual contact. Some, for instance, can come through parents, our children, or bosses. A soul tie is someone having the ability to control your thoughts, or deeds by simply being in your life. But, since we're talking about relationships, let's focus on toxic Ex's.

The more we battle these demons, trying to get over the person, the more we think about that person, causing us to want them more. And, since we normally want what we can't have, or shouldn't have, we crave it with fervent passion. Which only makes it more desirable to us, only placing us in a vulnerable position where we could make even more poor choices.

The only way to purge ourselves of our Ex's is to go cold turkey - completely NO CONTACT. No responses to their calls, text, emails, door knocks, or car horns. And, absolutely no contact from you to them via any of these channels mentioned above. No Contact = No Contact at all. No last romp in the hay. Not even if it's the best you've ever had. The point of no contact is to strengthen you where you're weak, build you up where you're torn down. Its purpose is to create in you a clean heart and renew the right spirit within you. It gives you time to adjust and focus. It allows you room to grow and become a better version of yourself.

Chapter 8

Letting go, is one of the greatest lessons you'll ever learn in life. It's not until we let go of the bad, that we receive the good. Oftentimes, we hold on so long to bad things, bad people, bad memories, or bad emotions that we get use to the bad in our life - to the point where if any good happens we're suspicious of it. Learn to let go of the bad, there's so much good just waiting to attach itself to you. In a nutshell, the chosen man that God has for you isn't going to come until you rid yourself of the longing, memories and daydreaming of your toxic Ex. God isn't going to allow a good man to have to suffer for what a bad man did to you. Remember, an Ex is an Ex for a reason - don't be afraid to use the Exit door.

While you're in the no contact phase, this is the time to ask for forgiveness of The Father (Abba Father) for any wrongs, or sins you've committed. Use this time to reflect on things you may have said, or done that you could of handled better. Humble yourself and repent. Not only reflect and repent, but also redirect your focus on the things of God. Ask God what would He have you do. Usually, the thing that you're supposed to be doing is the thing that brings you the most joy. God, what is my purpose? Your purpose is solely tied to that thing you would do for free without blinking an eye - because it's in you to do it.

So, while you're purging from all of the toxic energy, don't forget to refill yourself with positive energy.

Chapter 9

Preparation: Making it do what it do, until you say "I Do".

It's one thing to want a thing, it's quite another to actually be prepared when it comes.

This includes - but not limited to:

1. Regular Check Ups.

2. Yearly Mammograms.

3. Cooking healthier meals.

4. Regular Exercise.

5. Pampering Yourself.

6. Taking Up New Hobbies.

7. Living Adventurously.

8. Getting Rid Of Bad Habits.

9. Money Smarts.

10. Letting It Go.

1. Regular check ups:

What good are you to someone else if you're no good to yourself. Truth is, and it's not selfish thinking, but no one wants anyone who's constantly sick, or having one health crisis after the other. That's not to say that people with disabilities, or preconditions are not marriage material. On the contrary, many people have gotten married in spite of their current health state. But, truth be told, a person with multiple health conditions isn't at the top of the most wanted list. That's why it's vital (pun intended) that you have regular health check ups in order to know exactly what's going on with your body - so that you can start taking care of those things that are going wrong with your health.

2. Yearly mammograms:

No explanation needed. Just do it. It could save your life. Self checks are good. But, you need those puppies mashed down in a uncomfortable position to see what's really going on inside. Don't avoid any pain that you may feel, swelling, dents, or discoloration. Seek professional help if you sense that anything is off. If you have a pet that keeps on sniffing around a particular area on your body, don't shun them away, have that area looked at by a Doctor and always get a second, or third opinion. Animals have an uncanny ability to detect when something's not quite right - they can smell cancerous cells. Get it? Got it? Good.

3. Cooking healthier meals.

Well, unless you're planning on living off of junk food throughout your marriage - you'd better learned how to live healthy, so that you'll have a long and happy marriage. "Til Death Do Us Part" should have some years behind it - you shouldn't be rushing to push up daisies simply because you're not eating a well balanced meal. So, it would be wise to start practicing your culinary skills beforehand. Heck, use your family and friends as guinea pigs, or test subjects, whichever one better describes the situation. The good thing is, no one can drop dead twice - so that's a plus. LOL. Start out slow, boil some water and if that goes well, toss in some spaghetti. You got this, Girl. Good food may not win his heart, but it'll keep him around a bit longer. Ditch those reservations, stay home and make a home cooked meal.

4. Regular exercise:

First of all, don't get me wrong, exercise isn't about anyone else finding us appealing, that's not why we should be exercising on a regular basis. Our health and strength should be our first priority each day.

Don't do it for a man, do it because you want to be at an optimal performance level for yourself. No one wants to do it, but it must be done. Let's face it, we're not going to see the gains, or the six pack that we've dreamed of sitting on the couch surfing through channels, noshing on nachos, cookies, or candy and washing it all down with diet soda. We must make it a daily practice to exercise. Exercise releases endorphins into the blood stream that boost your energy and give you a better countenance, or positive energy. Exercise is the best way to combat stress, depression, high cholesterol, hypertension, fatigue, diabetes and cancer - along with numerous other health conditions. Exercise pulls oxygen into your blood stream and that's good news for your internal organs. Simply inhaling and exhaling (preferably outdoors) does wonders for your entire body - even your skin. Yes, regular exercise can clear up the skin as well, because the oxygen purifies the blood. That's why it's best to exercise outdoors, as opposed to indoors where the air is stagnant, or being manipulated by artificial air. And if we must go shallow, exercise just helps you look better overall. And who doesn't want a fit and toned physic, or a revenge body to showcase to the masses - or those people who secretly have animosity towards us. So flex your toned arms and sport those killer calves in your favorite pair of heels. But, putting the shallow end to the side, regular exercise aids in longevity and that is what's most important.

5. Pampering yourself:

Girl, now really, how could you not appreciate the gift which is you. It's fine to do for others, it's noble - it's Godly even. But, even God wants us ladies to attend to ourselves and go all out every once and a while. Whether you go to a health spa, or health resort, or simply fill your tub with hot water and your favorite bubble bath soap - surrounded by scented candles, it's all good, as long as you're able to relax - relate - release the stress. In this rare moment you should close your eyes and exhale, breathe out all of the stress that has build up over the course of days, weeks, or months. Afterwards, pour some wine (optional), lay on your clean, crisp white sheets and read a book, or listen to soft jazz music. Hopefully, you're able to do all of this without chaos running rampant in the other rooms. Just to make sure, take the rugrats to Grandma, or Auntie Barbara Gene (that one aunt who's more like a mama than an aunt) and allow yourself some sound me time. Learn how to meditate properly, no distractions - which includes no cell phone, or social media. Simply close off your space, sit quietly, close your eyes and breathe deeply - deleting the unnecessary images you've stored away in your mind, which only serve as reference points to when you weren't living your best life.

6. Taking up new hobbies:

Doing something that you've always wanted to do, but was always too busy. Painting. Gardening. Journaling. Collecting books, stamps, coins, babydolls - ants (LOL). Whatever it is, make it yours. Hobbies take our mind off of things - like, unnecessary drama, work, bills - men. Ha! Go on a mini vacay. Go to a museum, or planetarium to take in the beauty of nature. Learn something new, like mechanics, pottery, rock climbing, or learn how to play a instrument. It's all about not allowing your hands to become too idle. Because, we know what can happen when we're bored sitting around the house. Our idle hands start to pick up phones and dialing numbers we ain't got no business dialing, or texting. Put the phone down, Becky, it ain't worth it and you'll end up regretting it. Get out of the house, do something constructive, keep your mind and hands busy. Volunteer with a charitable organization in your area. It's a known fact that when we help others it diminishes depression and makes us feel good about ourselves. And when we feel good about ourselves our lives improve on every level.

7. Living adventurously:

Hold your horses, I'm not saying find a equally miserable friend and become Thelma and Louise. I'm saying finding that courageous person on the inside of yourself and becoming that daredevil who's unafraid of doing the craziest, wildest things. Such as, skydiving, paragliding, mountain climbing, horseback riding, kayaking, white water rafting, deep sea diving, swimming with the dolphins, etc. You may find, that after exploring other interest, you may not want to be bound down by wedding vows and the demands of marriage. Marriage? What marriage? I'm going snorkeling. Right? Right. Don't just live your life waiting to die - actually thrive in the life you have to live. Live life more abundantly, prosper in all good things you set your hands to do. Yes, run with the bulls if you must, just don't trip and fall, because that would be most unfortunate. Dare yourself to be the best you that you can possibly be - without needing bail money.

8. Getting rid of bad habits:

Are you a smoker? Stop. You're killing yourself, others and the environment with pollution. Ask yourself, do I truly love me, as a person, do I truly love my family as I claim. If you wholeheartedly love yourself and your family - quitting something that's causing damage to your body isn't hard. Just do it.

Are you a alcoholic? Stop. You're damaging your liver, your body's filtration system. And, you're causing damage to your overall health. You're loosing respect from family, friends and co-workers. Besides, no one likes a drunk - they just tolerate you. Recognize that you need help, then seek out that help. Addiction and Alcohol Hotline 1-855-399-4951 24/7. Alcoholism is a real problem in the westernized culture. Everywhere you look there is a commercial placating to the propaganda of alcohol. It's truly a bad habit to have. Alcoholism not only destroys the person who consumes it regularly, but those around them are equally effected. With the lies, excuses, job loss and even arrest records for DUI - all these things effect the entire household. If you find that you have to consume alcohol on a daily basis, it's time to seek professional help. You deserve to have a fighting chance at life - don't throw it all away for a demon in the bottle. No. I'm not the judge of you, but I care about you. And, if I, a total stranger cares about what happens to you - your family and friends should at least have a fighting chance of being with you a little longer.

Whatever it is that has you bound, work on putting those demons to rest for good. Baby steps - start slowly with the simplest of thing and progress as you see yourself moving past a particular vice.

9. Money Smarts:

This is going to help you out a lot. When you're able to put a handle on your spending habits - you'll be able to conquer many of your financial problems. This by far, is one of most crippling problems we as a people in western culture have today. Being unable to save money for those rainy days. Most households spend more money than they take in monthly having to borrow from Paul to pay Peter and giving Thomas a promissory note. And, considering that most marital problems stem from money issues, it's no wonder that the divorce rate has tripled. But once you've lassoed that "I've got to have that" urge, the battle is halfway won. Girl, just stop it. No. You don't need those shoes, that hand bag, or that little black dress - even though it's half off with an additional 20% off at the counter - but I digress. It's best to conquer this before your husband comes along - or else, divorce court will be in your near future. Men are able to put up with a lot of our foolishmess; But, driving him and the household into the poor house isn't one of them. Get it together, Mimi. You can control yourself better than that. It's either that man you've always prayed for, or those nice pair of red bottoms. And, although those red bottoms are nice (really nice), hella nice, I mean for real for real, it's more enjoyable to have a pair of nice strong toned thighs lying next to you in bed. Girl, listen here, don't get me started, I'll save that for another book. LOL. We'll talk - off the record in another love and relationships book.

10. Letting It Go:

Girl, LET IT GO. This needs to be reiterated from the purge section because it is extremely important that you understand how imperative it is to move passed yester-year. Holding on to old things, old memories - old lovers, serve no purpose but to stimulate your flesh. Bring your flesh under submission with prayer and fasting. "This kind goes out only by prayer and fasting" ~Yushua. How in the world do you expect to move on if you're still carrying old broke down luggage into the present. "Bag Lady, you gone hurt yo'self draggin' all those bags like that" ~Erykah Badu. It's high time to get rid of all those things that are weighing you down - all those ungodly soul ties gotta go. Why are you holding on to it, to them? Is it because it's familiarity. Or, you think that maybe it'll spring forth new life? (all rhetorical questions - of course). When the question was posed, "can these bones live again" - resurrecting dead matters and/ or toxic relationships wasn't in the equation. Girl, leave it all behind and KIM (keep it moving). Understand, Yahweh isn't going to send your husband until you've willingly removed all of that funky junk and access baggage out of the way. Look, you can't put new wine into old wine skin - it'll all go bad. So stop trying to get Lazarus to come out of tomb, he's dead for real this time - that old relationship that you wanted so badly can't be resurrected. Don't put your life on hold hoping that they come back. Don't make the mistake of waiting for them to leave their new lover - that they quite possibly left you for. Turn that joker loose mentally and step into your glorious future without him. Patterns don't change, if they mistreated you throughout your relationship with them, it›ll only continue once you've taken them back. And, if they come back, and they always do eventually, don't fall for the love bombing. The only reason they're back is because the new supply saw their mask fall off revealing what was truly underneath - the monster they hid within.

Chapter 10

All I'm saying is, be prepared for that great man Yahweh has for you and you can't do that holding on to a phantom. Trust me, your man is preparing himself for you also. But, don't forget while you're preparing yourself for him, get busy loving yourself, so that if it's not in your book of life to have that one true love - you'll be too busy loving on yourself and helping others that it doesn't really matter anyhow.

Bonus Tip:

Meanwhile, and in between time. Live your life. Be happy. Turn on the song by Pharrell "Because I'm Happy" and let that be your theme song. Dance. Sing. Laugh. You don't need to wait on another soul to enjoy your life. Life is this present moment right here in this time and space. Life is reality. Rejoice in it. Be grateful for it. Appreciate your life - right here where you are. Live out loud - be the best version of yourself. Look in the mirror and tell yourself, "I'm fearlessly and wonderfully made and Dear, God - I'm alive". Be sure to make that dash in between your birth date and your death date count.

National Council on Alcoholism and Drugs Dependence, Inc.
1-800-622-2255

CPA/Accountants
1-800-837-5160
scrubbed.net

National Suicide Prevention Lifeline
1-800-273-8255
SuicidePreventionLifeline.org

Planet Fitness
1-844-880-7180

Silver Sneakers
1-866-584-7389

Golds Gym
1-877-776-4777

The Spiritual Covering isn't meant to be a guide for how you should conduct yourself in a relationship. We all know that there are no ABC's, or 123's in matters of the heart. The Spiritual Covering is a vitamin to be administered whenever you find yourself needing a little extra boost of energy to get passed the rough spots in your life, as it relates to relationships.

I dedicate this book to those who are my biggest supporters and inspiration.

Darius E. Frazier
David E. Dawson
Al E. Walker
Thomas B. Zackary
Michael Motley
Dana Brinson
Gary Rohadfox
Anthony Colbert
Damaso Amaro

Author
Re'Dina L. Frazier

Reader's Notes

Reader's Notes

Printed in the United States
By Bookmasters